The Carver Policy Governance Guide Series

The Policy Governance Model and the Role of the Board Member
A Carver Policy Governance Guide, Revised and Updated

Ends and the Ownership
A Carver Policy Governance Guide, Revised and Updated

The Governance of Financial Management
A Carver Policy Governance Guide, Revised and Updated

Adjacent Leadership Roles: CGO and CEO
A Carver Policy Governance Guide, Revised and Updated

Evaluating CEO and Board Performance
A Carver Policy Governance Guide, Revised and Updated

Implementing Policy Governance and Staying on Track
A Carver Policy Governance Guide, Revised and Updated

T0307927

Praise for the Policy Governance Model

"Reading these guides is a great way to start your journey towards excellence in governance. All the essentials are there, short but clear. And these six guides will also prove to be an excellent GPS device along the way."

—Jan Maas, PG consultant, Harmelen, The Netherlands

"The guides are a great way to introduce busy board members to the basic principles of Policy Governance. Their bite-size approach is inviting, covering the entire model, albeit in less detail, without overwhelming the reader. They are succinct and easy to read, including practical points of application for board members. Consultants asked to recommend initial reading about the model can do no better than these guides."

—Jannice Moore, president, The Governance Coach™, Calgary, Canada

"Boards introduced to Policy Governance quickly become hungry for information but are short on time. These guides help board members quickly absorb the key principles of the Policy Governance model. They are invaluable."

—Sandy Brinsdon, governance consultant, Christchurch, New Zealand

"For some board leaders the governance elephant is best eaten one bite at a time. The Carver Policy Governance Guide series provides a well-seasoned morsel of understanding in a portion that is easily digested."

—Phil Graybeal, Ed.D., Graybeal and Associates, LLC, Greer, South Carolina

"Would you or your board benefit from a quick overview of essential governance concepts from the world's foremost experts on the topic, John and Miriam Carver? Thanks to their new six-booklet series, you can quickly familiarize or refresh yourself with the principles that make Policy Governance the most effective system of governance in existence. These booklets are the perfect solution for board members who are pressed for time but are dedicated to enhancing their own governance skills."

—Dr. Brian L. Carpenter, CEO, National Charter Schools Institute, United States

CARVER
POLICY GOVERNANCE®
GUIDE

Evaluating
CEO and BOARD
PERFORMANCE

Revised and Updated

JOHN CARVER
MIRIAM CARVER

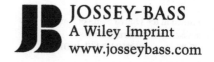

JOSSEY-BASS
A Wiley Imprint
www.josseybass.com

Copyright © 2009 by John Carver and Miriam Carver.

Published by Jossey-Bass
A Wiley Imprint
989 Market Street, San Francisco, CA 94103-1741   www.josseybass.com

No part of this publication may be reproduced, stored in a retrieval system, or transmitted in any form or by any means, electronic, mechanical, photocopying, recording, scanning, or otherwise, except as permitted under Section 107 or 108 of the 1976 United States Copyright Act, without either the prior written permission of the publisher, or authorization through payment of the appropriate per-copy fee to the Copyright Clearance Center, Inc., 222 Rosewood Drive, Danvers, MA 01923, 978-750-8400, fax 978-646-8600, or on the Web at www.copyright.com. Requests to the publisher for permission should be addressed to the Permissions Department, John Wiley & Sons, Inc., 111 River Street, Hoboken, NJ 07030, 201-748-6011, fax 201-748-6008, or online at www.wiley.com/go/permissions.

Readers should be aware that Internet Web sites offered as citations and/or sources for further information may have changed or disappeared between the time this was written and when it is read.

Limit of Liability/Disclaimer of Warranty: While the publisher and author have used their best efforts in preparing this book, they make no representations or warranties with respect to the accuracy or completeness of the contents of this book and specifically disclaim any implied warranties of merchantability or fitness for a particular purpose. No warranty may be created or extended by sales representatives or written sales materials. The advice and strategies contained herein may not be suitable for your situation. You should consult with a professional where appropriate. Neither the publisher nor author shall be liable for any loss of profit or any other commercial damages, including but not limited to special, incidental, consequential, or other damages.

Jossey-Bass books and products are available through most bookstores. To contact Jossey-Bass directly call our Customer Care Department within the U.S. at 800-956-7739, outside the U.S. at 317-572-3986, or fax 317-572-4002.

Jossey-Bass also publishes its books in a variety of electronic formats. Some content that appears in print may not be available in electronic books.

Policy Governance® is the registered service mark of John Carver.

Library of Congress Cataloging-in-Publication Data

Carver, John.
  Evaluating CEO and board performance: a Carver policy governance guide / John Carver and Miriam Carver.—Rev. and updated ed.
    p. cm.—(The Carver policy governance guide series)
  ISBN 978-0-470-39256-0 (alk. paper)
  1. Chief executive officers. 2. Boards of directors. 3. Directors of corporations. I. Carver, Miriam Mayhew. II. Title.
  HD2745.C37225 2009
  658.4'2—dc22
                                                                          2009003150

Printed in the United States of America
REVISED AND UPDATED EDITION
PB Printing   SKY10071447_040124

E veryone seems to be busy. Board members read materials and crowd board and committee meetings into their personal and business lives. Staff members report to work daily, and many leave tired when it's time to go home. Computers compute, transportation transports, and all manner of special machinery hums continuously. It all looks impressive, seems well intended, and runs as if it had a life of its own. But does all this admirable activity actually work? How do we know we aren't all fooled by our own busyness? Is everything happening that should? Is anything happening that shouldn't? Is the staff spending its time wisely? Are employees adequately trained? Are we paying too much for rent? Are there any off–balance sheet transactions going on? Is the board using its scarce availability well? Is it being a good employer? Is it spinning its wheels?

There are people at every level from board to upper management to frontline staff working hard with the intention of doing good jobs. The board, at the very top of the heap, not only wants to know whether all those jobs add up to something right and honorable but is legally and morally accountable that they do. It is no wonder that board members are continually worried about the weight of this accountability. In this Guide, we address the board's need to know whether the board itself and its operational organization are getting their jobs done.

As important as evaluation is, it is only one part of a total systematic view of governance. The upside of that integrated view is that every part makes more sense in the light of the whole. The downside is that no single question can be answered properly unless the whole is understood.

Therefore, we encourage you first to read the Carver Policy Governance Guide titled *The Policy Governance Model and the Role of the Board Member* for an overview of the Policy Governance model. For the reader who doesn't have that Guide, here is a brief summary.

Policy Governance in a Nutshell

- The board exists to act as the informed voice and agent of the owners, whether they are owners in a legal or moral sense. All owners are stakeholders but not all stakeholders are owners, only those whose position in relation to an organization is equivalent to the position of shareholders in a for-profit corporation.

- The board is accountable to owners that the organization is successful. As such, it is not advisory to staff but an active link in the chain of command. All authority in the staff organization and in components of the board flows from the board.

- The authority of the board is held and used as a body. The board speaks with one voice in that instructions are expressed by the board as a whole. Individual board members have no authority to instruct staff.

- The board defines in writing its expectations about the intended effects to be produced, the intended recipients of those effects, and the intended worth (cost-benefit or priority) of the effects. These are *Ends policies*. All decisions made about effects, recipients, and worth are *ends* decisions. All decisions about issues that do not fit the definition of ends are *means* decisions. Hence in Policy Governance, means are simply not ends.

- The board defines in writing the job results, practices, delegation style, and discipline that make up its own job. These are board means decisions, categorized as *Governance Process policies* and *Board-Management Delegation policies*.

- The board defines in writing its expectations about the means of the operational organization. However, rather than prescribing board-chosen means—which would enable the CEO to escape accountability for attaining ends—these policies define limits on operational means, thereby placing boundaries on the authority granted to the CEO. In effect, the board describes those means that would be unacceptable even if they were to work. These are *Executive Limitations policies*.

- The board decides its policies in each category first at the broadest, most inclusive level. It further defines each policy in descending levels of detail until reaching the level of detail at which it is willing to accept any reasonable interpretation by the applicable delegatee of its words thus far. Ends, Executive Limitations, Governance Process, and Board-Management Delegation policies are exhaustive in that they establish control over the entire organization, both board and staff. They replace, at the board level, more traditional documents such as mission statements, strategic plans, and budgets.

- The identification of any delegatee must be unambiguous as to authority and responsibility. No subparts of the board, such as committees or officers, can be given jobs that interfere with, duplicate, or obscure the job given to the CEO.

- More detailed decisions about ends and operational means are delegated to the CEO if there is one. If there is no CEO, the board must delegate to two or more delegatees, avoiding overlapping expectations or causing confusion about the authority of the various managers. In the case of board means, delegation is to the CGO unless part of the delegation is explicitly directed elsewhere, for example, to a committee. The delegatee has the right to use any reasonable interpretation of the applicable board policies.

- The board must monitor organizational performance against previously stated Ends policies and Executive Limitations policies. Monitoring is only for the purpose of discovering if the organization achieved a reasonable interpretation of these board policies. The board must therefore judge the CEO's interpretation, rationale for its reasonableness, and the data demonstrating the accomplishment of the interpretation. The ongoing monitoring of the board's Ends and Executive Limitations policies constitutes the CEO's performance evaluation.

Finding Out What We Don't Know

To delegate, as it must, the board has to set out its expectations for the CEO's job, and to have effective governance, it must set out expectations for its own job. Setting out expectations is a prerequisite for checking performance, for those expectations form the criteria for evaluation. Since the board is accountable for the organization, it would be irresponsible to allow others to make decisions with authority the board has handed out without checking that the authority was used in accordance with board expectations. Giving away authority without checking on its proper and effective use is not delegating but abdicating.

Throughout these Guides, we use the word *evaluation* to include both monitoring and self-evaluation. We use *monitoring* to describe the board's checking on performance of the operational organization. If you prefer other terms, like *reporting*, *evaluation*, or *perfor-*

mance appraisal, that is fine. We treat these words as interchangeable as long as they all mean checking against board-stated criteria. We use the term *self-evaluation* to describe the board's checking on its own performance.

Board members are always interested in finding a good evaluation method. They need a way to know, in view of the overwhelming number of available facts about governance and operations, what they need to keep up with in order to check on performance. It is folly to try to keep up with everything, even though you may know board members who believe they should do exactly that. And it is rather risky to keep up only with what squeaks or to keep up with a collection of board members' special interests.

You know, of course, that there is almost an unlimited amount of information available in the organization. What bits of the information available does the board need in order to check on performance? To make sense of the flood of information from the perspective of a governing board, it is best to think of information in three categories, each useful for a separate purpose. Only one of them is needed for checking performance, but using it requires board members to be able to separate it from the other two.

Decision Information   This category includes information the board needs in order to make wise, informed decisions. This is not information about the decisions the CEO or staff are to make; it is information for board decisions. It is not used to judge either the board's or the organization's performance but to prepare the board for decision making. It is nonjudgmental in the sense that no one's performance is being evaluated. All boards, no matter how intelligent and accomplished their members, need this kind of information. Policy Governance boards spend a great deal of time acquiring it. Except perhaps for trend data about the past, decision information is focused on the future. It can be collected from any source that can supply it from inside or outside the organization. It is not related to the chain of command, so useful information can arise from any level in the organization. Based on decision information, the board makes the policies we have described. All boards need decision information, for they cannot govern responsibly without it.

Evaluative Information   This category is by necessity focused on the past. It is judgmental by its very nature. It allows the board to assess its own performance and that of anyone to whom the board has delegated, including, predominantly, the CEO. On receiving evaluative information, the board is not simply perusing facts or indulging its general interest; it is making authoritative judgments of whether some person or some group got the job done. Being fair as well as rigorous requires the information in this category to be criteria-related. Evaluation, therefore, is an act of comparison: it compares what the board got to what it said it wanted. That is a meaningless comparison in the absence of previously stated board expectations. In fact, it is not only meaningless but unfair. All boards need evaluative information, for they cannot govern responsibly without it.

Because assessing performance is largely an inspection of the past, it should be made as routine and brief as possible in order to minimize its backward-looking influence on the content of board meetings and the mentality of board members. This alone is reason enough for isolating this kind of information from all others.

So if you are a board member, remember your job is not to know everything going on in the organization. You can't really do so anyway, for there is—or should be—far too much for you to keep up with. But more important, since your job is to be governor, not encyclopedia, you should attend with a laser focus to the categories of information that have specific relevance to governance.

Incidental Information   This category covers information that is not related to any decision to be made by the board, as well as information that cannot be used to evaluate performance because no preexisting criteria have been established. In other words, it is information that does not rise to the definitions of decision information or evaluative information. Incidental information is what some might call "FYI." While incidental information is often interesting and perhaps even uplifting, listening to, reading about, or discussing this information is unrelated to getting the governance job done. Many staff and committee reports, presentations, and site visits, and in fact much of the traditional board's agenda, contain information that is only incidental to governance.

Keeping the Focus on the Right Kind of Information

This Guide focuses on evaluative information rather than the other two types. But separating the types is necessary to that focus. Decision information is relatively easy to separate from evaluative information. Indeed, incidental information can also easily be separated from the other two, though most boards aren't aware of the importance of making this separation and, as a result, complicate and in the end damage their ability to govern.

The problem is not that there is something bad about incidental information or that boards should never receive it. The problem is that it easily masquerades as decision or evaluative information, leading board members to think they've done their duty with respect to the mandatory when they've only indulged their interest in the optional. Sadly—this is a great impediment to good governance—most of what most boards get most of the time is incidental information. Processing this information in the board meeting can cause a board to mistakenly think incidental information is part of the board's work. The necessities of governance include gathering information and wisdom, processing it with appropriate study and debate, making decisions in precise categories, and subsequently judging performance data—not becoming enthralled or even distracted by information that contributes to none of these elements of governing. A useful tactic is to keep board meetings focused on the necessities of governance, and then adjourn for social or other optional interactions.

When incidental information is misperceived as decision information, it is normally because it actually is useful, but useful for decisions made by someone at a lower position, not by the board. For example, consider the board of a large developmental disabilities system becoming informed on how to make minibus or desk purchases. It would almost certainly be learning incidental rather than decision information, since surely the CEO or even lower staff make these decisions. Training board members in how to construct operational budgets is incidental to governance if, as would be the case if there is a CEO, budget construction is a skill exercised by staff. Over our more than forty-five years of combined experience with boards, we have learned that most board training, no matter how lauded as a value in itself, has consisted of teaching boards how to do the wrong things better than they did them before. Incidental information is often mistakenly thought to be decision information.

When incidental information is misperceived as evaluative information, it is normally due to the belief that evaluation can be done in the absence of criteria. Sometimes it is due to thinking that a mass of descriptive facts about what is going on in an organization constitutes monitoring performance. Sometimes the unspoken assumption is that more information is better than less, even if the "more" consists of hundreds of potential answers in desperate need of a few good questions. In any event, the result is that real evaluative information becomes drowned in obfuscation, even if well-intended obfuscation. Consider for a moment that all or virtually all the host of numbers in a standard management financial report are presented without the board's having set forth any criteria in advance about what would be acceptable performance, thereby making them incidental information. Consider, too, that all or most of the beautifully presented staff reports address no criteria the board has set. The same can be said for generic board self-evaluation questionnaires.

But as important as it is for board members to be cautious about incidental information, lest it destroy their ability to govern accountably, we are not saying that incidental information is off-limits to boards. Incidental information isn't bad, it is simply incidental to the job of governing. We find it understandable, for example, that many board members benefit from incidental information because it helps them to feel more connected to the organization. Other board members want incidental information for political reasons; they don't want to appear ill-informed when asked about this or that operational issue by voters or others. This is understandable as well, though we really think that board members must learn how to say, "I don't know," and to send questioners to the people who do know without embarrassment.

But because incidental information typically clutters and obscures evaluative information, we advise a straightforward treatment for the specific incidental information a board wants. A board might want to know about certain things even though it feels no need to control them (which would require policy about them). The board can simply describe the classes of information it wishes to be kept informed about. For example, a board might want to know about personnel changes in the top ranks of staff, planned public events, pending lawsuits, upcoming media coverage, or anything else for any reason that strikes its fancy. If it is truly the board that wants to know rather than one or two board members, then the board need only incorporate these items in an Executive Limitations policy that prohibits the board's being left in the dark about them. There are no criteria associated with these items (except that they not be withheld), and they are not being used for board decision making. They are still incidental but have been carefully designated and when received will be flagged as such. In this way, the content of this information will never be used to judge CEO performance, even informally, though its presence or absence will be.

The result of this fine tuning is not to outlaw incidental data but to prevent them from overwhelming, crowding out, or being mistaken for information a board absolutely must have to do its job. Board specificity about desired incidental information informs the CEO which nondecision and nonevaluative information must be gathered and given to the board. Without a board "just want to know" list, it is typical for CEOs to base their disclosure of incidental information on one or a few board members' interests. Since CEOs normally want to be responsive, they have to do a lot of guessing about what they assume board members want to know, frequently swamping the board with unnecessary information in an attempt to avoid omissions that might offend specific members.

> So if you are a board member, nothing blocks your access to any information as long as the board itself asks for it or gives blanket authorization for individual members to get what they want as long as the cost of answering individual requests doesn't exceed some cost limit.

This situation—in rare cases, we trust—can be used by a less honorable CEO to befuddle a board with a hundred points in order that board members more likely overlook the few that would disclose failure to perform. We are amused by the complaints we sometimes hear from boards that they only find out what the CEO chooses to tell them. Of course they do. But that victimhood is self-imposed. The CEO has to select what to tell them if they have not identified what it is they want to know. And if the board has made itself clear and still has the same problem, it is time to remember who works for whom.

So while the Policy Governance model is very specific about the kinds of disclosures the board must have for proper monitoring, it is indulgent about what the board wishes to know just for the sake of interest. The board can know anything it wants as long as the just-want-to-know items are always clearly distinguished from monitoring information.

The Charade of Board Approvals

Before we describe what evaluation looks like in Policy Governance, let's briefly look at the approach taken by typical boards who are not using Policy Governance. We've made a point that one cannot make sense of evaluation unless expectations for performance have already been set. We emphasize this point because although boards always agree this sequence makes sense, actual board practice rarely follows the rule. When we look at what passes for evaluation in boards not using Policy Governance, we find boards examining documents or activities but comparing them to few or no criteria at all. Let us examine one common instance.

Boards have a common practice, as you are aware, of examining financial reports prepared by management on a regular basis. Usually the report is presented to the board with some narrative provided by the CEO, the chief financial officer (CFO), or sometimes a board member, such as the treasurer or finance committee chair. After a period of discussion, a motion is made to approve, accept, or receive the financial statements (the terminology varies). The board then indicates its assent. With respect to the board's role, *approve, accept,* and *receive* all, in their effect, mean the same thing. If you were to ask why the board had gone through this process, undoubtedly you would be told that the board has a fiduciary responsibility to determine whether the organization's finances are OK. That is true, of course, but the standard approval process is a poor way of fulfilling this duty.

On occasion, after a board has approved a document with hundreds of numbers, we've asked if board members found all the numbers acceptable. Following some consideration, they explain that some of the numbers matter hardly at all, while some are crucial. Asked which of the numbers are crucial, boards stumble for an agreed-upon answer. In other words, *as a board*, they have had no idea which are the indicators (such as liquidity) that matter to them. But even if they did, they also have no idea what amount of, say, liquidity is too much or too little. Their approval would seem to indicate they've pronounced the document to be OK, despite not knowing *as a board* what it

So if you are a board member and you've ever thought there's just too much in this report to know honestly whether you approve or not, trust that instinct. Being overwhelmed by information is one of the signs of having negligible or incomplete criteria to go on.

should show or should not show. Yet according to accepted practice, they have taken an official action that professes to be the exercise of fiduciary responsibility.

But let us take this to the next obvious step. If we ask board members after an approval of financial statements what would have caused them not to approve, the result is normally a stunned silence. Granted, individual board members sometimes do have clear ideas for themselves about what would cause a financial statement to be unapprovable. But individual board members are not the board; the non–Policy Governance board has rarely designated with one voice those aspects of financial management it wants to control and therefore ones for which criteria must be set. The fact is that financial statements contain numbers that reflect thousands of decisions, all of which have already been made. It is hard to know what the effect would be if the board withheld its approval! In the end, the board has judged as acceptable a very important organizational means with no previously stated criteria or, worse, it has merely agreed that the last month or quarter existed.

We are encouraged that among some lawyers, there may be a trend toward board approvals to be worded more like "the board finds the report to demonstrate reasonable compliance." That would be an improvement over a simple "we approve," but deciding a document is acceptable in the absence of clear board statements about what unacceptable looks like still means that the board's approval is a procedural veneer. We know that this "approval syndrome" is time-honored and tradition-blessed, frequently required by regulations or funders, but it demeans the crucial board obligation for fiduciary responsibility.

Board approvals of staff documents such as budgets and program plans and board documents such as committee reports fall into the same category: they declare work to be acceptable even though board members have no performance criteria established by the board to use in making that judgment.

Criteria-Focused Evaluation

The Policy Governance model, then, requires boards to make a clear distinction between the common practice of granting approvals and the more precise and fair practice of monitoring against criteria. This one feature of Policy Governance transforms so much about the way boards think and the way CEOs relate to boards as to render boards' former practices indefensible. Because it is so important to understand the difference between approval and monitoring, let us present two scenarios as further illustration. For these scenarios, we use board-CEO examples, but the same principles apply to board-CGO or board-committee evaluation, since any time the board delegates authority, it must carefully attend to fulfilling its accountability for how the authority is used.

Consider scenario A, in which, following traditional procedure, the CEO, at considerable cost, develops a proposal that requires board sanction. It is sent to board members; they conscientiously study it and come to the meeting with questions. Board members ask their questions in turn, and the CEO tries to answer these questions to the satisfaction of each questioner. The CEO can only guess what board members will ask about or object to—that is, what individual members might treat as their own personal criteria on which to base their opinions. If the CEO gives satisfactory answers to enough members, the proposal is likely to be approved. Note that in this process, the CEO has to please board members one at a time. The CEO is working for a collection of individuals, not the board's one voice. Even if the proposal is approved, the board has established no criteria about the matters contained in it. This means that future similar proposals will have to be put through the same process: no new

So if you are a board member, it may be easier to characterize the familiar board approval method as "poke and probe" and the Policy Governance approach as "define, demand, and disclose."

knowledge about board requirements has been added. If the proposal or report was not approved, then we can assume that something in it was so contrary to board members' values that whatever it was caused the submitted item or whole proposal to be deemed unacceptable. Wouldn't it have been helpful if the board's criteria about what it would not accept had been known by the CEO in advance? What a lot of wasted effort would have been saved.

Contrast that process with scenario B, wherein the Policy Governance process is in place. The board, recognizing and priding itself on being a collection of people with diverse values and perspectives, learns about, debates, and eventually decides its group values in the form of policies. In this case, we are referring to Ends and Executive Limitations policies, for they establish the job description of the organization: what is to be achieved and what is to be avoided. The CEO will have been given the right to use any reasonable interpretation of those policies. At intervals of the board's choosing, the board requires evaluative information that would describe whether or not reasonable interpretations of the board's expectations have been met. The board then must determine if, totaling its separate members into one voice, as in all decisions, it is convinced that the CEO has passed this test. Board members who wanted the criteria to be different must reach their personal decisions based on what the board policy is, not on what they wanted it to be, for to do otherwise would be an abuse of position.

> So if you are a board member, express your personal opinions about how the organization should operate in terms of ends and unacceptable means when board policies are being created. But when reviewing monitoring reports, those opinions are irrelevant. The only judgment for you to make is whether a reasonable interpretation of what board policies actually say has been fulfilled.

Since the board's expectations were known in advance, the likelihood of their being met is significantly increased. After all, we all know that it is more likely that we will get what we want if we say what we want than if we don't. Also, because the CEO knows the criteria on which his or her work will be judged, that judgment is fair rather than a "gotcha" exercise. Further, because the board knows it is being fair, it need not soften the rigor of assessing performance. Also, monitoring against a finite but inclusive set of criteria enables monitoring performance to move quickly. Without criteria to focus the board's inspection, examining the past is more difficult, more time-consuming, and more inconsistent; it is simply easier to find what you want if you know what you are looking for. Moreover, a criteria-focused concentration reduces the likelihood of board members, who are human, after all, treating the CEO as if he or she has either halo or horns. The board owes the ownership rigorous objectivity and is bound by simple ethics to be fair. In the Policy Governance approach, both values are served.

All this sounds as if the board judges nothing except what it has already controlled in its policies. That is exactly what we mean. Otherwise, governing proceeds without careful consideration of what must be controlled and therefore what can be left uncontrolled. Under such circumstances, governance comes to be a capricious process of creating personal criteria on the fly, not group criteria up front. All this may sound as if the board's work must be done before it makes any sense at all to evaluate the CEO. That is exactly what we mean. Governance is a front-end job; after all, that is what leading requires. This kind of board leadership, leading the parade instead of bringing up the rear, describing the organization's job in terms of expected achievement and conduct, causes the board not to be so much the *final* authority, as we often hear, as the *initial* authority.

> So if you are a board member, keep in mind that a decision made with authority that the board has delegated is as genuine a decision as if it were made by the board itself. There is no need for the board itself to make a decision in order for that decision to be authoritative.

The Policy Governance insistence on exclusively criteria-focused monitoring is revolutionary to many boards, but in other settings, it is a familiar practice. Physicians regularly compare blood test results to preestablished ranges. The ranges themselves have been given great thought and debated ahead of time. Data for a specific individual would be of little use without the criteria with which to compare them. Consequently, medical judgment can be made with a quick perusal.

Having discussed principles of evaluation common to the board's monitoring of CEO performance and its own self-evaluation, we will discuss these two evaluations separately. We begin with the monitoring of CEO and organizational performance.

Monitoring CEO and Organizational Performance

Whether a board chooses to use a CEO function or not, to use Policy Governance it still must define the organization's job (ends are accomplished, unacceptable means do not occur). The main reason to use a CEO function is that it allows the board the advantage of being able to hold one person accountable for the organization's performance. Hence the CEO is accountable not for the accomplishment of his or her own personal contribution to the total but for the total itself.

Remember, when we say "CEO," we mean a position defined in a certain way. We are not concerned with the title the CEO is given. The function we call "CEO" is the first single executive below the board and over all operational staff, paid or unpaid. It is possible, then, for the CEO to have any of the titles we are accustomed to: general manager, executive director, president, superintendent, and so on. It is also very common for a person with one of these titles to not really be a CEO.

Just as with other board decisions, the board records in policy its decisions on its approach to monitoring. The same policy can also detail the board's intended monitoring method and frequency.

Exhibit 1 shows a sample policy titled "Monitoring CEO Performance" that would be placed into the Board-Management Delegation policy category. Titles of policies to be monitored as well as monitoring method, frequency, and specific months of monitoring are up to each board; those shown here are merely examples.

Exhibit 1. Board Policy on Monitoring CEO Performance.

Policy Category: Board-Management Delegation

Policy Title: Monitoring CEO Performance

Systematic and rigorous monitoring of CEO performance will be solely against the only expected CEO job outputs: organizational accomplishment of any reasonable interpretation of board policies on Ends and organizational operation within the boundaries established in board policies on Executive Limitations, reasonably interpreted.

1. Monitoring is simply to determine whether or not expectations expressed in board policies have been met. Information that does not disclose this will not be considered to be monitoring information.

2. The board will obtain disclosure about the CEO's interpretations of the board policy being monitored from the CEO him- or herself.

3. The board will obtain data disclosing whether or not the CEO's interpretations have been accomplished using one or more of three methods:

   a. By internal report, in which the CEO discloses the data to the board

   b. By external report, in which an external, disinterested third party selected by the board collects the data

   c. By direct inspection, in which data are collected by the board, by a designated board member, or by designated board members

Exhibit 1. Board Policy on Monitoring CEO Performance, Cont'd.

4. In every case, the board will determine the reasonableness of the CEO's interpretations, using a "reasonable person test" rather than interpretations favored by board members or the board as a whole. The board is the final arbiter of reasonableness. The board will also assess whether data demonstrate the accomplishment of the interpretation.

5. All policies that instruct the CEO will be monitored at a frequency and by a method chosen by the board. The board can monitor any policy at any time by any method but will normally use a routine schedule.

Policy	Method	Frequency	Month
Actual Financial Condition	Internal	Quarterly	1,4,7,10
Financial Planning	(a) Internal (b) External	(a) Annually (b) Annually	(a) 3 (b) 10
Treatment of Staff	Internal	Annually	6
Asset Protection	Internal	Semiannually	2, 12
Compensation and Benefits	Internal	Annually	6
Communication and Support to the Board	Direct inspection	Semiannually	1, 7
Ends 1 [by whatever title]	Internal	Annually	2
Ends 2 [by whatever title]	Internal	Annually	9

Monitoring CEO performance requires two components of evaluative information in order to demonstrate performance of a reasonable interpretation of board policy: first, since the CEO is authorized to use any interpretation of board policies that is reasonable, he or she must disclose what his or her interpretations actually were, along with the rationale for their reasonableness. Second, the board must receive data that describe the CEO's degree of accomplishment of the interpretation.

The CEO's Interpretation

The language of the board's Ends and Executive Limitations policies may not be measurable, but the language of the CEO's interpretations must be. Although the "any reasonable interpretation" rule exists to recognize and harness the fact that instructions are open to interpretation whether we like that fact or not, the other benefit of the rule is that it forms a natural bridge from the nonmeasurable to the measurable. That is why, using Policy Governance, there is never a need for a board to worry about the measurability of its policy language. It is not at all uncommon for a board to back away from requiring meaningful organizational outputs because it sees them as hard to measure.

Many rich board discussions have been truncated because a board member stymies the group with "How are we going to measure that?" Under Policy Governance, the board can thoughtfully pursue the most meaningful expression of its demands even if it has no idea how it can be measured. In fact, stopping that fertile process, perhaps the most valuable gift boards have to give, to wrestle with measurability is destructive. It is not the policy that gets measured anyway but the CEO's interpretation of that policy.

Since interpretations are what will be measured, then clearly the interpretations must be explicit, measurable, and not simply restatements of the policy or dictionary definitions of it. CEO interpretations are best constructed in the same way as operational definitions in research.

We describe operational definitions more in the Carver Policy Governance Guide titled *Adjacent Leadership Roles: CGO and CEO*. Briefly, the term means the interpretation of a more general concept or idea in a measurable way. For example, a CEO might operationally define literacy for tenth graders as a score greater than the 75th percentile on the XYZ Reading Comprehension and ABC

Writing Tests. Whether that is a reasonable definition or not is for the board to decide, based on the CEO's stated justification, but you can see that something relatively vague becomes very concrete and measurable in one stroke. The operational definition idea is borrowed from scientific research, where it is a common practice. With this approach to gathering knowledge, anything conceivable becomes measurable.

So if you are a board member with subject matter expertise, remember the CEO is not required to make the interpretation you would have made. However, the reasonableness of the CEO's interpretation should be obvious from the description of his or her rationale.

In addition, the asserted reasonableness of these interpretations must be justified. "It's reasonable because I said so" is not a justification. We encourage CEOs to justify their interpretations carefully so that the board is in no doubt as to their reasonableness. And we urge boards to remember that they have allowed the CEO to use *any* reasonable interpretation of the applicable policy. We will give some examples of CEO interpretations when we present sample fragments of monitoring reports.

It might be useful if we point out that the CEO needs to interpret—that is, operationally define the board's policies—upon receipt of them. Thinking up interpretations when it's time to submit a monitoring report is a bit late. We see the work flow from board policy to monitoring report shown in Figure 1.

Figure 1 shows that the CEO needs to have interpreted board policies in order to formulate plans, design organizational structures, and further delegate responsibilities. This is a time-consuming process without which subsequent demonstration of fulfilling board-stated expectations is impossible. But take care that your board does not write policies for the sake of writing them. Overcontrol imposes a huge monitoring burden on the CEO, who has to interpret and measure potentially unnecessary policies, and on board members, who have to read and evaluate the reports. You should take care that your board imposes only the minimum necessary policies, not the most possible policies, on the operational organization. The pur-

Figure 1. The Cycle from Policy to Monitoring.

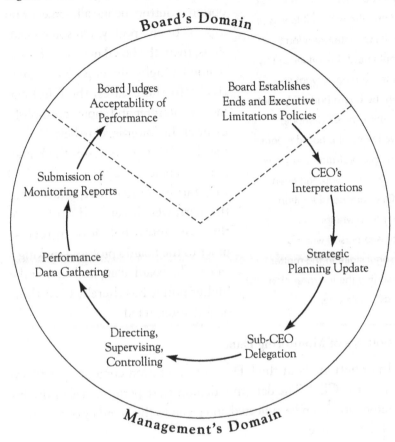

Note: The cycle begins with board establishment of ends and executive limitations policies and terminates with board receipt and judgment of both the reasonableness of the CEO's interpretation and the credibility of performance data.

pose of an organization is not to spend most of its time creating reports. Just because something can be controlled does not mean it should be. The "any reasonable interpretation" rule will prevent overcontrol if you use it carefully.

Here is a tip regarding the CEO's interpretations. The creation of board policies proceeds from a broad statement of the board's expectations to a more narrowly defined level, then possibly to another level, and so forth to the various "any reasonable interpretation"

So if you are a board member, judging the reasonableness of the CEO's interpretation should never be influenced by what you meant, what you wish the board had said, what you think the CEO should have known the board meant, what interpretation you would have made if you had been CEO, or any consideration other than whether an unbiased person with no personal stake in the matter would find the interpretation a reasonable one.

points. The board at each level has the option to further define all, some, or no aspects of any policy. On some occasions, then, the board may have further defined a higher-level policy exhaustively. In these cases, the CEO can merely interpret and show accomplishment of the lower-level policies, knowing that doing so addresses the higher policy completely. Therefore, the CEO can start his or her interpretations at the narrowest levels and work up to the more broad policies—in reverse order to the board's process—making a case to the board, if applicable, that the higher policy has thereby been thoroughly interpreted.

Sources of Monitoring Data

Information about the CEO's interpretation comes to the board from the CEO. The data that demonstrate performance of the interpretation can be collected and given to the board by one or more of three sources.

CEO Report Unless the board has chosen one of the next two sources of monitoring data, the "default setting" is the CEO report, also called the internal report. Data are collected by the CEO or by persons under CEO authority, whether staff or outsiders on contract. This is the most common source of monitoring data used by boards, and it is usually the cheapest. But it suffers the disadvantage of an appearance of self-interest.

External Report The possibility of self-interest leads boards to have data collected by persons not under CEO authority. These data collection agents must be appointed by the board, for if chosen by the CEO, they automatically become instruments of the CEO. The advantage of this source of data is that it is independent of management influence; the disadvantage is that the cost is normally higher. The familiar independent audit is one of the external report methods. We must reiterate, however, that even though the data collection is done by an agent of the board, rather than of the CEO, the interpretation of board policies is still the CEO's prerogative.

Direct Inspection   The third option for the board to acquire monitoring data is by collecting the data itself. We do not recommend this method except in rare cases. Data collection by boards is a cumbersome process, and data collection by designated subparts of boards such as committees or officers seems to invite these subparts to add "on the fly" extra criteria to be met by the CEO. This potential undermining of the board's one voice is risky.

So if you are a CGO, setting the frequency for monitoring each Ends or Executive Limitations policy is as simple as asking, for each policy, how many board members think monitoring once per year would be OK, then how many think twice per year would be OK, and on down to monthly. When the cumulative OKs passes the 50 percent point (or whatever criterion the board sets), that is the monitoring frequency.

Frequency of Monitoring

Monitoring performance is necessary, of course. But monitoring too frequently imposes an unnecessary cost, and monitoring too infrequently diminishes board control. The frequency of monitoring CEO performance against Ends and Executive Limitations policies is established by the board and can be altered any time by the board. In other words, the board monitors as often as it chooses, whether on a regular schedule or sporadically. Typically, a board will decide the frequency and method (CEO report, external report, direct inspection) that it will routinely use, noting these decisions in a Board-Management Delegation policy. This routinizes the monitoring; but despite setting a routine schedule, the board reserves the right to monitor any policy by any of these methods at any time.

Because both the preparation of monitoring reports and the reading of them are time-consuming, we suggest that the board decide on the lowest frequency of monitoring that it can agree is prudent. There is no point in monitoring more often than necessary. Policies that control volatile aspects of the organization are normally monitored with more frequency, while others are monitored less often. Further, there is no need for the monitoring schedule to coincide with the board meeting schedule. Reports can be sent to board members when due, irrespective of whether there is a board meeting scheduled at the same time. However, the board formally deals with the report when it does meet.

> So if you are a board member, proper monitoring is worth doing well, but it does cost resources. So adding unnecessary detail to policies is wasteful, since it increases the cost of monitoring.

We have often been asked if it is necessary to be so rigorous about monitoring board policies. Our view is that there is no point in imposing requirements on an organization if checking to see that they were met is not taken seriously. A policy worth stating is worth monitoring.

If you refer back to Exhibit 1, you will see an example of the Board-Management Delegation policy used by many Policy Governance boards to describe the expectations they set for themselves about monitoring.

The Monitoring Report

At this point, we present examples of portions of internal monitoring reports. You will note several features: the CEO attests to the veracity of the information presented; the CEO repeats the words of the board's policy to accommodate board members who may not have their policy manuals at hand; the CEO's interpretations are measurable and justified as to their reasonableness; in the case of ends monitoring, the CEO's interpretations of the board's Ends policy are themselves ends, not descriptions of the means to be used; and finally, data are presented to demonstrate the accomplishment (or not) of the interpretation.

Partial Monitoring Report

Unspecified Organization

Quarterly Internal Monitoring Report: Executive Limitations Policy on Treatment of Staff

I certify that the information contained in this report is true.

[*signed by the CEO*]

Board Policy: The CEO will not cause or allow employees to be subjected to unfair conditions of work.

CEO Interpretation: Using the opinion of legal counsel, union leadership, and various online HR resources to support these interpretations, and upon administration of an anonymous questionnaire to a random sample of employees, or upon examination of a random sample of employee files, it is necessary to find that:

1. 90 percent of respondents agree that they know the rules of the workplace or can easily find out what they are.

   Rationale: Employment attorneys and union leaders consulted agree that it is inherently unfair if employees are subjected to rules of which they are unaware. Ninety percent attainment is reasonable given the usual and expected level of inattention to management communications among employees as reported by the [*reference source*].

2. 95 percent of employees report that they have the tools and resources they need to do their jobs.

   Rationale: Legal counsel and union leadership confirm that unfairness could be alleged if this requirement is not met. Ninety-five percent is reasonable given the likelihood of there being a small percentage of our five hundred–strong staff who consider the resources provided by management to be inadequate whatever they might be. This is consistent with the findings of the [*reference source*].

3. 100 percent of files demonstrate that performance appraisals have been conducted for employees within the last thirteen months.

   Rationale: It is unfair to expect employees to know how their performance is rated or how to improve it unless they are told, according to legal counsel and the National Institute of [*name here*].

4. 100 percent of employee files contain evidence that the employee has received the booklet "The Grievance System: How to Use It."

Rationale: Employees who are unaware of how to complain about their conditions of work or about management decisions will experience the workplace as inherently unfair, according to union leadership and our attorney.

5. 90 percent of respondents should report that they are unaware of any employee encountering negative consequences such as poor performance appraisal or job reassignment to less favorable hours as a result of the use of the grievance system.

Rationale: Employees who fear that reprisals will result from grieving work conditions will deny themselves the use of this protection according to legal counsel and union leadership. Ninety percent is the required high level of agreement since despite the inevitable frustration of employees who may not win a grievance, it is important that the vast majority of employees have faith in the integrity of the grievance system.

Data submitted, based on questionnaire in March and file examination March 20:

1. 91 percent

2. 94 percent

3. 90 percent

4. 99 percent

5. 94 percent

The questionnaire used has a margin of error of plus or minus 2 percent. Accordingly, I report compliance for all interpretations except item 3. Compliance with item 3 will be accomplished within six weeks.

Partial Monitoring Report

Professional Society

Annual Internal Monitoring Report: Ends Policy on Member Skills

I certify that the information contained in this report is true.

[signed by the CEO]

Board Policy: Sufficient to justify the expenditure of 50 percent of the society's annual resources, members will have the business skills necessary for successful practice.

CEO Interpretation: Fifty percent of available resources on an annual basis is approximately $[*amount*]. Following a consultation with randomly selected members grouped into two categories (practitioners in single-person or small offices of fewer than six persons and members running larger group practices), it was learned that members in small practices identify the need to learn basic bookkeeping and salary administration skills, while members running large practices identify the need to improve their skills in supervision of and delegation to clerical staff. Given the available resources and using the information provided by [*credible source*] about the cost of producing these skills, I intend that in each of the next three years, it will be demonstrated through the use of questionnaires that:

1. Fifty (50) members will learn the basic principles of bookkeeping to their satisfaction.

2. One hundred (100) members will learn the use of the XYZ bookkeeping software to their satisfaction.

3. Seventy-five (75) members will have the skills to accurately handle payroll, making the required reports and payments to government, to the level that they encounter no staff complaints or government imposed fines for overdue filings.

4. One hundred twenty-five (125) members will learn basic management principles about delegation to office staff, including matters relating to customer relations to their satisfaction.

5. One hundred (100) members will learn the skills necessary to supervise junior members and office personnel to their satisfaction.

   Rationale: The skills described here are those members themselves defined in a questionnaire in November of last year. Levels of accomplishment are judged worth the resources expended based on data provided by the [*credible source*].

Data:

1. 52

2. 100

3. 75

4. 127

5. 120

I report compliance.

Judging the Report

When board members receive monitoring reports, they are obliged to read them. Unlike incidental information, this is not optional, since board members have to assess the adequacy of the information presented. Each board member has to answer for himself or herself the two questions that follow. The individuals' answers are then combined in a judgment made by the board as a body about the CEO's performance on the policy criteria in question.

First Question: Is the Interpretation Reasonable? Each board member must ask "Am I convinced that the CEO has made reasonable interpretations of this policy?" This is a very different question from "Do I like the interpretations?" "Do I agree with the interpretations?" "Are these the interpretations I expected?" or even "Would I have made these interpretations if I had been CEO?" It is also different from asking "Is this what we meant?" The CEO was not asked to guess what the board *meant*. He or she was required to make reasonable interpretations of what the board *said*. Asking whether or not it has been shown that the interpretations are reasonable is the only fair question.

We urge CEOs to provide justifications for their interpretations so that there is no chance of a dispute about their reasonableness. In practice, if clear justifications are provided, we have found that usually there is no such dispute. However, if the majority of the board, in carefully applying the "any reasonable interpretation" rule, is not convinced that the interpretation is reasonable, performance on the policy in question must be ruled out of compliance no matter what data are presented.

Second Question: Do Credible Data Show Accomplishment of the Interpretation? If the board member finds an interpretation reasonable, the next question to be answered is "Am I convinced that these data demonstrate the accomplishment of the interpretation?" In seeking the answer, it is important to be sure that the data really are data and not simply assurances, plans for compliance, or stories about how much work is being done toward compliance. Obviously, in order to be convinced, the board member must find the data credible. If the board member and eventually the board as a body find that the CEO has made and accomplished a reasonable interpretation of the applicable policy, the CEO has passed the test.

Board Reaction to Reports

We are often asked if a finding of out-of-compliance performance should result in the board's altering its policy. We can think of few reasons why it should. As you can see, unless the policy was undoable in the first place, out-of-compliance performance tells the board something it really needs to find out. It reveals whether the CEO is getting the job done. Just as we don't change a law simply because it was broken, the board doesn't change its policies due to failure to perform.

Finding a lack of compliance, as will occasionally happen in the real world, calls for careful exercise of board judgment. Not all out-of-compliance situations are catastrophic; in fact, most are not. The board needs to know about them but need not take drastic steps in response. The board should not attempt to help fix the situation, as this is the CEO's job. Neither should it get involved in the CEO's plan to fix things. The board's concern should be *that* the out-of-compliance situation is fixed, not *how*. But it should decide, with CEO input as necessary, how long it will have to wait to see restored compliance. Naturally, some substantial out-of-compliance situations, as well as accumulations of several smaller such situations, could prompt the board to decide that it has the wrong CEO. This is part of the judgment boards are obligated to exercise. But in no event should lack of compliance simply be overlooked.

> So if you are a board member, the CEO's job is to convince you that a reasonable interpretation has been accomplished. So as long as you are unconvinced, you must vote that the policy has not been fulfilled. It is not your job to do anything other than apply your "intelligent generalist" talent.

But what if the board finds the CEO has made a reasonable interpretation, but that interpretation is not acceptable to the board? In this case, the board has erred, not the CEO. The board said that its policy depth was sufficient so that any reasonable interpretation would be acceptable when actually it was not. This situation calls for amending the policy while commending the CEO's performance. This circumstance can happen if a board isn't thoughtful enough in writing the policy to begin with, if the environment has changed but gone unnoticed, or if board members or their values have shifted since the policy was written. That it can happen argues for a board's always keeping its policies current; they are working documents.

So if you are a board member, recognize that accepting blame for inadequate policy may be difficult. But take no risk that the CEO might be seen as responsible for a board error. This is one of those times when being a board member requires moral courage.

At each board meeting, we suggest that the board have an agenda item in which board members confirm receipt and review of monitoring reports due since the last meeting. After discussion, usually brief, the board should agree to a motion that indicates its finding that the CEO did or did not achieve a reasonable interpretation of the policies being monitored. Such decisions are recorded in the minutes to establish a record of due care.

What is the role of monitoring in the overall evaluation of the CEO? For this question to come up means either the CEO role or the purpose of monitoring has not been clear. Monitoring organizational performance for which the CEO is accountable—that is, monitoring Ends and Executive Limitations policies—*is* the CEO's performance appraisal. Policy Governance boards usually monitor these policies at least once a year; when the time comes for the CEO's annual evaluation, they know that evaluation has been occurring throughout the year. What else is to be monitored? The policies contain all the expectations for the CEO's performance expressed by the board. If anything else were to be added, it would have to be previously unexpressed expectations, an unfair and inconsistent approach to governing. In its effect on organizational performance, annual CEO evaluation is not nearly as valuable as the continual policy-by-policy monitoring we've explained.

Board Self-Evaluation

Let's start by considering the reason for doing any self-evaluation at all. It's not really so the board can have a self-produced report card so much as so the board can continually improve its performance. Evaluation of the board makes it more likely that the board will follow its own rules than might be the case without continual reference to those rules. That is what board self-evaluation is about: continual comparison of what the board does and produces with what it said it would do and produce.

Again, just as with CEO performance, evaluation must always be against previously stated criteria. So self-evaluation by the Policy Governance board is always based on the policies in categories that control board actions and outputs: Governance Process and Board-Management Delegation.

Policy Governance contains principles that, though easy to understand, can be hard to follow, at least at first. Old habits die hard, and the habits of traditional governance are no exception. Boards using the model must employ a great deal of group discipline in order to be predictable to the CEO, as well as generally coherent and model-consistent. Self-evaluation is a major way in which this group discipline can be established and maintained.

Self-evaluation against the expectations stated in Governance Process and Board-Management Delegation policies is so crucial to maintaining board discipline that we suggest engaging in it on a very regular basis: at least once per meeting. We do not mean interminable periods of introspection. We mean brief, to-the-point evaluations of the board's compliance with its own policies. There are a number of workable ways to do the evaluation, but we are not aware of one best way. Depending on the level of policy detail a board has gone into in describing its commitment to self-evaluation, the method will fall to the board or to the CGO to decide. In most cases we've found, boards leave it to the CGO and his or her reasonable interpretation of what the board has said. Here are some examples we've seen of boards' keeping themselves on track:

- Read aloud at the start of the meeting from one Governance Process and one Board-Management Delegation policy.

- Ask a board member, a different one at each meeting, to conclude the meeting by reporting back to the board on its compliance with its own policies.

- Select a group of board members to act as meeting monitors, giving them the right to interrupt the meeting if the board goes off track.

- Ask the really picky board member to be really picky about the board's governance process and give feedback about it.

- Use the services of a thoroughly trained Policy Governance coach.

We have not seen a necessity for board self-evaluation to be carried out with the precision and rigor required for CEO monitoring, mainly because there is less to evaluate in the board's job than in the CEO's; it is simply less complex. But we do recommend that the board self-evaluate often and always against its policies. This will maintain board skill and consistency even without a scorecard.

Conclusion

We have argued in this Guide that the board is required to evaluate the performance of the organization as well as its own governance performance. Our focus has emphasized the necessity for evaluation to be based on previously stated criteria that when operationalized are measurable. We have pointed out that the principles of the Policy Governance model enable a board both to demand performance from its organization and itself and to determine if its demands were met.

About the Authors

John Carver is internationally known as the creator of the break-through in board leadership called the Policy Governance model and is the best-selling author of *Boards That Make a Difference* (1990, 1997, 2006). He is co-editor (with his wife, Miriam Carver) of the bimonthly periodical *Board Leadership*, author of over 180 articles published in nine countries, and author or co-author of six books. For over thirty years, he has worked internationally with governing boards, his principal practice being in the United States and Canada. Dr. Carver is an editorial review board member of *Corporate Governance: An International Review*, adjunct professor in the University of Georgia Institute for Nonprofit Organizations, and formerly adjunct professor in York University's Schulich School of Business.

Miriam Carver is a Policy Governance author and consultant. She has authored or co-authored over forty articles on the Policy Governance model and co-authored three books, including *Reinventing Your Board* and *The Board Member's Playbook*. She has worked with the boards of nonprofit, corporate, governmental, and cooperative organizations on four continents. Ms. Carver is the co-editor of the bimonthly periodical *Board Leadership* and, with John Carver, trains consultants in the theory and implementation of Policy Governance in the Policy Governance Academy.

John Carver can be reached at P. O. Box 13007, Atlanta, Georgia 30324-0007. Phone 404-728-9444; email johncarver@carvergovernance.com.

Miriam Carver can be reached at P. O. Box 13849, Atlanta, Georgia 30324-0849. Phone 404-728-0091; email miriamcarver@carver governance.com.

Notes